HOMES AROUND THE WORLD

Anna Sproule

Macdonald Educational

How to use this book

First, look at the contents page opposite. Read the chapter list to see if it includes the subject you want. The list tells you what each page is about. You can then find the page with the information you need.

If you want to know about one particular thing, look it up in the index on page 31. For example, if you want to know about longhouses, the index tells you that there is something about them on page 26. The index also lists the pictures in the book.

When you read this book, you will find some unusual words. The glossary on page 30 explains what they mean.

Series Editor
Margaret Conroy

Book Editor
Margaret Conroy

Production
Susan Mead

Picture Research
Diana Morris

Factual Adviser
Sarah Hobson

Reading Consultant
Amy Gibbs
Inner London Education Authority
Centre for Language in Primary
Education

Series Design
Robert Mathias/Anne Isseyegh

Book Design
Julia Osorno/Anne Isseyegh

Teacher Panel
Peter Denman
Lynne McCoombe
Ann Merriman

Illustrations
Lorraine Calaora Pages 6-7, 10-11, 12, 13, 23, 28 left, 29 right
David Eaton Front cover
David Salariya Pages 8-9, 17, 20-21, 24-25, 26-27

Photographs
Cover: street scene in Cameroon

Associated Press: 13
Douglas Dickins: 14
Greg Evans Photo Library: 7 top, 22
Richard & Sally Greenhill: 16-17
Alan Hutchison Library: cover, 15, 17, 18-19, 19 bottom
Homer Sykes: 13
UNHCR/photo Jean Mohr: 14-15
ZEFA: 7 bottom, 9, 19 top

CONTENTS

PEOPLE

What is a home?

Home means different things to different people. Living at home might mean living with your family. But if you live in a house or a flat on your own instead, that is still your home.

Your home is where you sleep at night. It is also where you keep your things, where you eat most of your meals, and where you meet the rest of your family.

In some parts of the world, people live in tents or boats, or in homes made of wood and grass, or even in drainpipes. None of these is a house or a flat, but all of them are home to someone.

Ever since people lived in caves, home has been a place where people feel safe enough to enjoy themselves.

Some people still live in caves today. These cave-houses are in Turkey.

You can get out of the rain at home. You can also get away from people that you don't want to be with. People don't usually come into your home unless you invite them in.

To begin with, thousands of years ago, people lived in caves. That was where they could protect themselves and their children from the dangers around them. Even today, being without a home is still a frightening thing. It means not knowing where you are going to sleep every night. It means not having a place to go where you feel safe.

Happy at home: an old lady watches TV with all her treasures around her.

7

People in towns

We all need to eat, drink, sleep and have somewhere to live. In some parts of the world, people grow their own food and build their own houses. But in many places they have to use money to buy food and to buy or rent a home.

For nearly everybody the only way to get money is to work for it, so most people live near where they can find work. Today many people go to towns or cities to find paid work.

A town often starts for just one reason. Some towns start because they are in a good place for a port, or there is a coal mine or a gold mine nearby. A town grows because there is some particular work to be done there.

The workers who go to live in the town usually take their families with them, and they all need things like shops, hospitals and schools. So there are even more jobs to be done, and more people who need somewhere to live. As the town grows, people may have to live further away from their work in suburbs around the edge of the town. Where does your family live and why do you think it lives there?

In the centre of a town, people often live very close to their work. The homes over the shops here are in India.

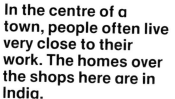

This town probably got much bigger when the railway was built. Shops, schools and hospitals were built for the people living there.

People in the country

Almost everything we eat was once grown by somebody living in the country. If there were no land to grow food on, there would be no food for ourselves nor for the animals that many of us eat.

Hundreds of years ago, when towns and cities were very much smaller, nearly everybody lived in the country, close to where food could be grown. They either grew their own food or worked for other people who grew it.

Many people still do this today. But in rich countries where farmers own a lot of modern machinery, the machines now do the jobs of farm-workers. So, many homes they once lived in now belong to people who do other sorts of work. Sometimes families from towns use them for holidays.

All farmers in rich countries grow food to sell, not just to eat themselves. Some farmers in poor countries can do this too, but many need all the food they can grow to feed themselves and their families. This is called subsistence farming.

The houses shown are all different although they all belong to farm-workers. Look how different they also are from homes in towns.

This farm is in Denmark. The farmhouse is old, but the farmer can afford to buy modern machinery. Most of the farm products will be sold.

Sugar-cane harvest in Jamaica. The sugar is sold to many other countries. Corrugated iron is often used for the roofs of the workers' small houses, which are raised above the ground for coolness.

West African women dig the ground, ready to plant the millet crop. Behind them are their homes in the village, and tall storehouses for the grain. Most of the crop will be eaten by the villagers.

People on the move

When they move into a new home, most families mean to stay there for several years. Sometimes — especially in the country — the family stays there for centuries.

But there are some people who make their living by always being on the move. They are called wanderers, or nomads. Many of the Indians of North America were nomads who moved around because they lived by hunting buffalo. Today, the Sami or Lapp people of the far north of Scandinavia move to follow their herds of reindeer. Gypsies are also nomads, as are many of the Mongol people who live in central Asia.

Two camels can carry the felt tent used by the Mongols. It is called a yurt.

The yurt's framework.

Putting on the felt.

The felt is firmly tied down, and the yurt is ready.

Living in a yurt.

The Mongols have enormous herds of cattle, horses, camels and sheep. These move around to feed, and the Mongol people move with them and keep them together. Gypsies often have horses too, but many of them are traders. They sell things they make or that they have bought from people they meet on their travels.

Most nomads take their homes with them on their journeys. They carry the things they need to live, such as rugs, blankets and cooking pots. They also take personal things which make their shelters into their homes. A lot of nomads live in tents, which are easy to carry and quick to put up. But in Australia the nomad Aborigines built shelters of materials they found where they stopped.

An Aborigine bark shelter. Today, nearly all Aborigines live in towns.

Gypsies with modern caravans still like to have camp fires.

People making do

All over the world, there are people who have to move around because they have no real homes. They live where they can. A lot of them live in places that nobody else wants. Sometimes, they cannot choose how long they will stay there.

Some of these people have been driven out of their old homes by a war and have become refugees. To get away from the fighting, they may travel to another country and then they often have to live in camps built specially for all the refugees like them.

Hundreds of refugees lived in this camp after a war in Cyprus.

These drainpipes are home for refugees in India.

14

People sometimes move from one town to another to find work. In the countryside, the poorest people often have to leave their homes when there are no farm jobs, or if bad weather spoils the food they grow for themselves. Then they have to earn some money somehow to buy food and so they go to towns to look for jobs.

These people often sleep on the streets when they reach the towns. Even the ones who find jobs probably can't afford to live in well-built houses. They make do with huts they build for themselves out of any materials they can find. There are huge groups of these huts on the edge of many cities. They are called shanty towns.

A crowded shanty town in South America.

PLACES

Living high up

People's homes look different in different countries. Even in one country, homes may look different from each other. But the homes in one particular part of that country can all look much the same.

The homes shown in the pictures here are alike in one special way. The people who live in them all live very high up.

The way your home looks often depends on the place where it is built. Buildings in a big town or city have to be tall and narrow because there are so many of them. There is no room for buildings to spread out sideways so they have to go upwards. People end up living on the twentieth floor or even higher.

But there are other reasons for living high up. One is to get away from enemies, and another is to keep out of the damp where there is marshy ground or ground likely to be flooded.

Hundreds of people live in these flats. There is not much room to play.

16

Homes are built on the mountainsides in Nepal.

A safe home on stilts in the islands of Melanesia.

Living by water

Would you like to live on a boat? A lot of people do. Sometimes they do it just for fun. Often, however, people live in floating homes because there is no room for them to live on land. In some cities in south-east Asia, boats are tied up next to each other in huge groups to make floating 'villages.' You can often see a small boat-village where a river runs through a busy town.

Some families who live in boats make their living by catching fish. So do a lot of people who live beside the water rather than on it. Other people earn money by buying and selling things that are brought in by boat from foreign countries. By trading like this, the people who lived long ago in the Italian city of Venice became very rich.

Venice is built on a group of islands and mudbanks. The first Venetians were refugees who came to the islands hundreds of years ago to get away from their enemies. The city grew as they built homes on the mudbanks.

All the houses stand on big underground posts driven deep down into the mud. Because there is not much room, the buildings are squashed tightly together.

Everything is done by boat in Venice — even bringing food to market.

Boat-village in Ho Chi Minh City in Vietnam.

The water would have to rise very high to flood these South American homes.

Living with danger

Long ago, life was very dangerous for almost everyone. Rich people built castles with thick stone walls to protect themselves. When enemies attacked, poor people took shelter there too.

People still have enemies and there are still wars. But nowadays life is also dangerous in other ways. The places where we live can be made unhealthy by pollution from smoking chimneys or petrol fumes from cars and lorries.

We can prevent this by making laws against pollution, but there are places in the world where there is no pollution and these can be dangerous in ways we cannot prevent. Some places are cold and windy. Others are threatened by earthquakes or volcanoes. Places near rivers or seas may get flooded. Whenever they can, people try to build homes that will protect them from such dangers.

Some building materials can make houses dangerous. If a stone house falls down in an earthquake, the family inside may be crushed to death, so in places where there are many earthquakes, homes are often built of very light materials. Then, if the houses fall down, the people inside will not be so badly hurt.

The high sills at the bottom of these riverside doorways keep out the floodwater. The doors open inwards behind the sills.

In some countries there are terrible storms called cyclones. This is Darwin, in Australia, after a cyclone in 1974. There is no water supply so people are being given soft drinks.

The pillars under this new Darwin home will let it sway on its foundations if another storm comes. Also, the wind will blow straight under the house, so that it is not knocked down.

BUILDINGS

Building for climate

All homes are alike in one special way. They are built to protect the people who live in them from the weather. This is done differently in different parts of the world.

In very cold countries, homes are often built of wood. This is because wood is a good insulator: it keeps the cold out of a house and the heat in.

Homes in hot countries are built to keep the heat out. Sometimes they have big windows that let breezes blow right through the building. Sometimes they are built round shady courtyards. The air in these becomes cool at night and stays cool in the daytime, so the rooms stay cool too.

A town in Afghanistan. Houses are built to keep out the Sun. They have few windows and are built around courtyards.

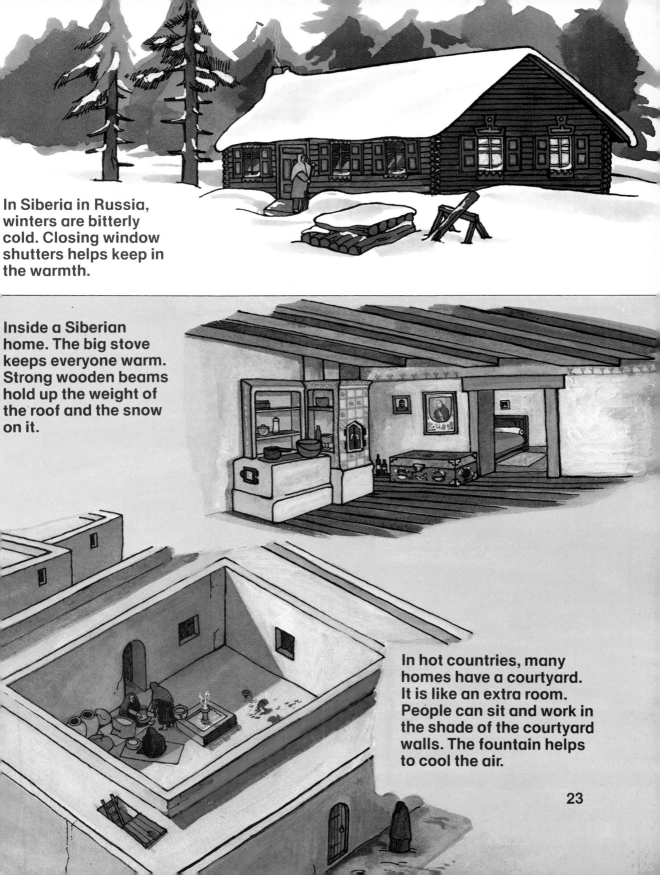

In Siberia in Russia, winters are bitterly cold. Closing window shutters helps keep in the warmth.

Inside a Siberian home. The big stove keeps everyone warm. Strong wooden beams hold up the weight of the roof and the snow on it.

In hot countries, many homes have a courtyard. It is like an extra room. People can sit and work in the shade of the courtyard walls. The fountain helps to cool the air.

23

What are homes made of?

All over the world, the homes being built for people today are often built out of the same kinds of materials. A block of flats in Birmingham can look just like a block of flats in Korea. Both are built of concrete and steel. But older houses are usually built of materials such as stone, bricks or wood.

Most people used to build their homes out of materials that were easy to find nearby. In some places, they still do. So, in places where there are a lot of trees, homes are often made out of wood. People use bricks to build in areas where there is clay to make the bricks.

This house of finely carved wood was built by Maoris in New Zealand.

In the marshes of Iraq, reeds grow up to 7 metres high. These pictures show how the Marsh Arabs use the reeds as building material for their homes.

The roof goes on the framework.

Cutting the reeds.

24

In Iraq, there are reeds that grow as tall as trees. People tie these reeds into bundles to make the framework for their houses. In Africa, some homes are made out of grass: it is tied into bunches and they are fixed over a frame to make a home shaped like a big beehive.

Another sort of home that was beehive-shaped was the Eskimo snow-house or igloo. If snow is packed hard enough, it can be cut into blocks like stone. The igloo was built from blocks going round and up in a spiral. Any gaps were filled with loose snow.

Eskimos made igloos when they were away from home on hunting trips. They used to live in tents in summer, and houses of wood and stone in winter.

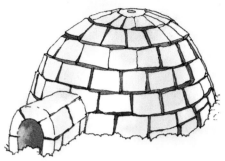

Eskimos used to build igloos like this on hunting trips. Most Eskimos now live in modern houses in towns or villages. The Eskimos' name for themselves is the Inuit.

Inside a reed house.

People at home

Next time you come home, pretend you have never been there before. Go into every room and look at it really carefully. How many things is it used for? Could it be used for anything else?

The way homes are built inside depends on how people want to use the space. It also depends on how rich they are, what materials are used for building, and the way that people live in that country.

Many people like to have a home of their own. Other people, sometimes several families, like to share a home between them. They all use some rooms, such as the kitchen, and have other space just for themselves.

This longhouse in Sarawak is like a whole row of houses under one roof. Each family has its own section with a room for sleeping and a cooking area with a fire and water supply.

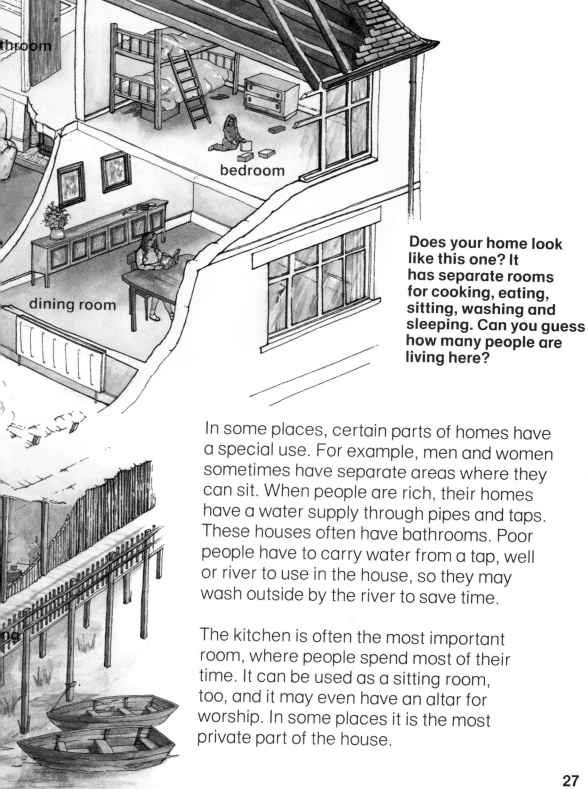

bathroom

bedroom

dining room

Does your home look like this one? It has separate rooms for cooking, eating, sitting, washing and sleeping. Can you guess how many people are living here?

In some places, certain parts of homes have a special use. For example, men and women sometimes have separate areas where they can sit. When people are rich, their homes have a water supply through pipes and taps. These houses often have bathrooms. Poor people have to carry water from a tap, well or river to use in the house, so they may wash outside by the river to save time.

The kitchen is often the most important room, where people spend most of their time. It can be used as a sitting room, too, and it may even have an altar for worship. In some places it is the most private part of the house.

Homes built to last

Homes made of wood, grass or snow do not last very long. Snow melts; wood is eaten by insects and rots in the damp; both wood and grass can catch fire. But they are all materials that are easy to find and build with. So, if a house is destroyed, the people that lived there can quickly build a new one. Some wooden houses are built slowly with great care and last a long time.

Another material that is easy to handle is dried mud. Skilled builders can make mud homes which last for hundreds of years. But rain and frost can damage them.

One way of building with dried mud: making mud bricks in Mali.

This fine brick house was built in England over four hundred years ago.

To make sure that a home will last a long time, it must be built of something like stone or brick. These are very strong materials. They are also more difficult to handle than grass or mud, and so homes made of them take longer to build.

Many old houses built of stone first belonged to very rich people. Long ago, only the rich could afford to buy stone and to hire people who knew how to build with it. But brick was cheaper and, after a while, both rich and poor people began to live in long-lasting brick houses. Today, long-lasting homes are often made from concrete. Building with concrete is both quick and easy.

Concrete is also long-lasting, and quicker to build with than brick or stone.

GLOSSARY, BOOKS TO READ

A glossary is a word list. This one explains unusual words that are used in this book.

Concrete Building material made by mixing gravel, sand, cement powder and water.

Cyclone Violent tropical storm. Places threatened every year by cyclones include Australia, the Caribbean, India and China.

Foundations Thick layer of solid material — rock or concrete — on which a house is built. Old houses have often been built without foundations. If they stand on soft ground, their walls can start to sag.

Insulator Material through which heat passes slowly. Wood is a good insulator and metal is a bad one. Good insulating materials keep heat inside a house.

Longhouse Malaysian building that contains homes for several families. As many as a hundred people can live in one longhouse.

Nomads Wandering peoples. They usually — but not always — look after herds of animals.

Pollution Anything which makes the world around us, such as the air, rivers or the sea, unpleasant and perhaps harmful to humans, plants and animals.

Refugees People who leave their homes because they no longer feel safe there. Usually this is because of a war, or a flood, or an earthquake.

Sami The name that Lapp people call themselves. They prefer the name Sami because 'Lapp' is often used against them as an insult.

Spiral Line that unwinds from (or winds in towards) a central point. A snail shell makes a spiral — and so does the line made by the building blocks of an igloo.

Subsistence farming Farming which only produces enough food to feed the farmer and family. No extra food is left to sell.

Suburb The edge of a town or city. It is usually an area which has mainly housing and little industry.

Yurt Collapsible home of Mongol nomads. It is made of felt stretched over a framework.

BOOKS TO READ

You can find out more about other people's homes in these books. Mos of them are a bit harder to read than this one. They all have good pictures.

City Life and **Village Life**, both by Olivia Bennett, Macmillan Education/Save the Children Fund and the Commonwealth Institute, 1982.

Deserts and People by James Carson, Wayland, 1982.

Houses and Homes by Carolyn Cocke, Macdonald Educational, 1976.

Living Together by Anna Sproule, Macdonald Educational, 1982.

Tundra and People by Ian Barrett, Wayland, 1982. This has a lot of information about Eskimos.

The World Around Us by Sydney Wood, Macmillan, 1982.